# 7 Steps
## to Repair
# Unhealthy Relationships

By
William Graham

*Earthly Stories with a Heavenly Meaning*

7 Steps to Repair Unhealthy Relationships
Graham, William

Published By Parables
April, 2021

All Rights Reserved. No part of this book may be reproduced or utilized in any form or by any means, electronic or mechanical, including photocopying, recording, or by any information storage and retrieval system, without permission in writing from the author.

    Printed in the United States of America

Readers should be aware that Internet Web sites offered as citations and/or sources for further information may have been changed or disappeared between the time this was written and the time it is read.

# 7 *Steps*
## to Repair
# *Unhealthy Relationships*

### By
### William Graham

# Introduction

Imagine you discover a dent in the side of your car. At first you are enraged by the thought of someone damaging your beautiful car deliberately. Now imagine you discover it was "you" who put the dent in the car. This is how we feel once we discover it is our fault we've damaged our relationships, and must take the proper steps to repair our unhealthy relationships.

I remember the day I turned 16 years old, for some odd reason I thought I was a full grown man or something. Just like most young males who start acting funny once they see hair growing in odd places on their bodies, I was no different. One day I was sitting on the school bus, when this kid who I knew was a senior at my school pulled up beside the bus in one of the most beautiful cars I had ever seen. To be honest with you I can't even recall what model car it was, but I knew it was nice and I wanted one for myself. Like a bat out of hell I rode my bike over to my cousin's house, who at the time owned a car repair garage. Personally I'm not a real car type of guy; I could careless about how cars functioned as long as they are clean and make me look good I'm satisfied. Anyway I recall begging my older cousin for a car of my own, I needed one bad. At first he fought me tooth and nail saying things like "you know you aren't ready to take care of your own car!" And "do you even you even have a driver license?" of course I lied through my teeth to get what I wanted, but hysterically I did not know how much work went into taking care of a car. I believe most of us misinterpret how much work goes into sustaining our relationships. Like for example if you don't like to communicate in your daily relationships, it's almost you are putting everyone you love on an island of lost translation.

William Graham

# Table of Contents:
*Consider what life has in store for you and your heart.*

Step One: Acknowledgements
Step Two: Accountability
Step Three: Honesty
Step Four: Comprehension
Step Five: Seeking Forgiveness
Forgiveness Letter
Step Six: Listen to Understand
Step Seven: Giving Them Time (Patience)
Now What?
The 6 R's of Repair
        Realization, Reliability, Respect, Reconciliation,
            Responsibility, and Rebuilding.

# Acknowledgements:

First I would like to give a warm thank you to my brother Ronald Frye and sister Suzanne Gomez, who embodies what it means to have a beautiful love book story relationship. Special thanks to Patricia Riley, my best friend and beloved family member for encouraging all my crazy ideas and supporting my ambitions. I would like to acknowledge Danielle Hudson who is a true lioness at heart. I also would like to give a special thank you to all my S.U.R.G.E teammates- Rory Atkins, Travis Barnes, Ahmad Nelems, Christopher Taylor, Louis Lopez, Sgt. Surge, Mr. Green, Mr. Shemar from Cross Purpose and all the positive members who support our noteworthy cause of change. Special thanks to my brother Nicholas Pacheco and the beautiful Kelly Bruce who gave me a heart to remember and a divine sense of purpose to admire. Christopher Miller and Desiree Miller, who gave insight to the challenging world of true love and understanding life. I would like to give a warm greeting to my mother Marilyn Boykin Frye, who has a heart of gold and reminds me to use my mind to understand life but use my heart to live through it. A brotherly embrace goes out to Nicholas Pacheco a.k.a Fingers, a dear friend and family member beyond any words or thoughts at hand. Thank you to Damon Davis, my brother, who has earned the birth right of a king in my book. Special warm hearted thanks to Louis Lopez and his beloved mother, Gina Lopez who have supported me and wrapped their arms around me in full embrace. I would like to thank my dear brother, Everett Michael Harrington, who inspires me to seek better and produce light even in dark situations. Special thanks to my older brother, Ceasar T. Graham, who showed me how to overcome losses and strive for greatness in life. Special thanks to Maykayla Scott for showing me how to have a beautiful heart and trust the process of understanding. Special thanks to DU PAI

(Denver University Prison Arts Initiative and Dr. Ashley Hamilton for all the endearing positive attributes and defining love. I would like to give a very beloved thank you to Pastor John Dee Jeffries, who granted me an opportunity of a lifetime and a blessing beyond words. A very special thank you to Albert Gallegos, who has a heart of gold and always strives for God's undying grace. I would like to give a special thanks to CDOC Director Dean Williams and God Behind Bars, Thank you to all the staff @D.R.D.C and D.W.C.F in Denver, CO and the nursing staff at both facilities. I must give a very warm thank you to the D.R.D.C library staff led by Ms. Bassford who provides a window of learning and possibilities beyond imagination. I would like to give a very special thank you to my son, Cyprese Lee Graham, for giving me a sense of purpose and legacy to cherish dearly. A thoughtful thank you goes out to Sean Marshall "SD", who told me to let the world see me in color. I would like to give a very special thank you to Vanessa Ann Harrell for having the power to grow beyond anything I could have ever imagined, I'm very proud of you. Thank you all.

*"When you look in the mirror and see yourself, trust all that you see"* -- **Sara Berry**

# Self-Reflection

One of the first steps of repairing unhealthy relationships is recognizing how important the relationship is to you. Speaking of the "you" factor, it is very important to identify the relationship you have with yourself before appreciating the relationship you have with others.
How do you feel about yourself?

_____

_____

How do you value your relationships? (Circle one)
    Poor              Average            Above Average

Why?
_____
_____


The main reason why self-reflection tugs at the heart strings of so many people is because evaluating one's self is a very difficult thing to do. Have you ever seen someone, whether at church or by the Xerox machine at work, who knew all the gossip? Every time you see this person they are more than happy to catch you up on the latest news involving someone else's life. The definition of self gives merit to a person or thing as an object of reflective introspection. The cold hard truth is most people are completely unaware of their own self-reflection. For example: I had this friend when I was fairly young whose hygiene wasn't always up to par, and to make it worst he played a lot of sports. I remember one time I tried to trick him into pointing out this factor. I ran up to him and lied saying someone said you smelled bad. (Sadly to say my efforts were denied by his funk). Just like my past friend who could not see his self-reflection most of us do not see our faults in the mirror as well. As we all know no one's perfect, but I challenge you not to use this as an excuse to neglect your faults or short comings, work on your self-reflection. Someone once told self-reflection is like looking in the mirror and seeing yourself differently than others see you. Like let's take a clown for example: when a clown looks in the mirror, an independent business person could be what the clown sees in them self, but to us a clown is still a clown right! I find it quite humorous when I look back at how I use to dress when I was young, with my sagging pants and big shirts 3x bigger than my normal size. Now I wouldn't be caught dead dressing like that anymore (why?) I grew out of it, and I noticed it wasn't my style compared to how I seen the world dressing. When we identify our true self-reflection we must be willing to appraise our uniqueness instead of conforming into what the world desires us to be. I remember my cousin telling me something very profound when I was young. He said "life copies itself already, but every thing has its own time." I'll be honest with you guys, at the time I considered my beloved cousin to a mad man who just enjoyed saying things to see if he could mess with my mind. But the truth is even wisdom has a time to come to pass for us to be able to digest its beauty. Ask yourself these questions and take a little time to ask those who know you best to elaborate on your outer reflection. It's very important to understand how others who love you perceive you as well.

What are my most admired qualities?
_____
_____

If you were to adjust something about me, what would you adjust?
_____
_____

Why?
_____
_____

Did you know wolves that join packs have to adhere to a certain order of hierarchy? I find that quite amazing how an animal allows itself to be graded by its own kind, and strives to meet a daily quota of required activities. What does that say about us as humans? As you exit this passage please keep in mind at times we forget how unique we are, and how important our self-reflection is to ourselves and others. Here are a few words on self reflection that I wrote a couple years back. I'm aware of how I should look because I desire to be seen the way I perceive myself in my mind. I'm conscious of why I feel certain ways at times because I understand feelings come and go as they should when evoked and acted upon. I'm positive I will make mistakes in life, I'm human, but I refuse to make excuses for why I can't adjust my vices that hold me back from being the best me I can be.

Let's say you had a mirror which always told you the truth no matter how horrible that truth seemed to be, could you handle hearing the truth all the time? Personally I believe a lot of people, when faced with their own ugliness, prefers to avoid it. Some individuals are so vain in their efforts to create a world where they win every battle; they refuse to face the truth regardless of where it comes from. It's very important we look at life from a different set of eyes if we truly desire to repair our unhealthy relationships. Here's the kicker about the whole self-reflection thing, which you've probably heard before. The truth about any self-reflection is there are two perspectives to consider. The first perspective is your own perception of yourself. (This includes how you see yourself? Also this includes how you desire to live your life and conduct yourself in your personal relationships.) The second perspective to consider is the perspective of those who look at you and judge you for what is presented. I know what you're saying to yourself, and normally I would agree with you. No one should live their life searching for the approval of others constantly, but there is a healthy sense of caring about how people see you. Let's say you believe yourself to be the nicest person in your neighborhood, but everyone thinks differently of you. I convey this information to you from a personal perspective, seeing how I use to think I was an alright type of guy. If you would have asked me 15 years ago if my perspective was jaded, surely, I would have been the first person to call you crazy. The truth being, like many others, we operate under the pressures of one way thoughts. If you are truly trying to grow beyond your past reflections, you'll desire to hear other's perspectives as well as formulate your own.

> *"The person who is owed the least expects the most"*
> **-- The Word Victim**

At times we find ourselves asking why we have to go through certain obstacles in life to seek happiness. We find ourselves worried about what tomorrow will give us or take from us in some cases. Insurmountable problems are the ones that force us to reflect over our lives and ask ourselves how much of my problems are from our own fruition? Like for example let's say you and your boss get into a heated argument about you being on time. Despite your explanation, I ask who is in the fault of this altercation. That's right, it's definitely you wearing the sign around your neck that reads (fired employee) not them. You do understand that right? And even though you probably had a legitimate excuse why you were late to work, but the truth is the relationship between boss and employee doesn't involve the word victim. I can't tell you how many times I felt like my care givers were wrong for putting me on punish for acting out in class. If you were to ask the 14 year old me if I thought they were picking on me I would have been the first one to tell you how unfair it seemed. When we examine the word victim we must be careful not to jump into shoes which are blame free. The self-reflection of blaming others has a way of excuses ourselves from the arches of blame. It is not healthy to ignore the blame jar once it gets passed around the room; everyone plays a damaging part in an unhealthy relationship.

*"Accept yourself first, and then search for individuals who reflect your thoughts and attributes. The moment you don't accept yourself is the moment you'll see yourself stuffed inside the broken mirror of other people's reflection."*
-- Denise Presson

# Jealousy

Let's say you have a friend who happens to be your co-worker as well. At first you two are the best of buddies, taking your lunch breaks together and talking on the phone about a collection of things. Then within a blink of an eye your friend gets promoted to a higher position in the company. Let's also say you've been trying to get this position your friend just got promoted to for the last 5 years now. It's evident you're not mad at the fact that your friend got the job, you're just mad that your friend doesn't have time to hang out with you anymore. To be honest with you it sounds like jealousy has seeped into your veins and gave you a purpose to hate your friend. But the truth is you're not mad at your friend about the promotion, you're upset with yourself for not working hard enough to get what you want out of life. Would you like to hear another real bold truth about life? No one owes you anything in this life, and you can't be upset about what you don't get from the work you don't submit. It's a common fact that people change all the time, sometimes for the better-sometimes for the worse. If you want something in life you have to be willing to fight for it like you'll die if you don't get it. If you're not willing to fight for the things you want in life, don't be surprised if no one hands you a free title or calls you champ.

*"You eat what you kill and complaining about what you don't have or what you feel you deserve wot feed you either"*
**-- Rory Atkins (Big 40 oz)**


## The Truth Is Bitter, but a Lie Taste Good

We gravitate to what we like to hear
As if our ears become deaf to reality
We love to be told a lie
Simply because we don't even have to try
Searching for the truth is hard
It's usually buried in our own backyards
Buried deep with all the broken scars
All the dirt
All the trick cards
Licking lies off the silver spoons taste good
Like missing pictures in frames of time
We don't always do what we should
Telling ourselves everything can't be swept under the rug
But we still pick up the broom
Lying to ourselves
Until truth walks into the room

William Graham

# Step One: Acknowledgement

As we acknowledge the damage we caused to our loved ones, its best we recognize how we hurt the bond. The first step is admitting you damaged the bond, and you need to try everything in your power to repair the bond. But the true reparation begins with "You" acknowledging you were wrong or you wronged someone you care about dearly.

Describe a relationship that you feel you have damaged and how would you repair it if possible?

_____

_____

Truthfully I can't tell you how many people I've met in prison who tried there hardest to convince me to buy into their nonsense. I swear to you I've heard it all; crying, complaining, yelling, pouting, silent treatments, dirty looks from afar, lying etc. etc. (it's as if people are upset when you don't buy into their hogwash.) With that said I say we damage relationships in many different ways, some of these ways are because we refuse to acknowledge our faults and short comings. Contrary to what you may believe to be true acknowledging a wrong doing is quite difficult. The truth is no one likes saying they're sorry, unless you're counting the cheaters on the Jerry Springer Show, they love saying they're sorry. For the rest of us prideful people, saying sorry feels like a dirty or vile word we must say when we've done something terribly wrong. I can't recall saying sorry for too much in my life until I committed my crime and found myself incarcerated years later. I'll be completely honest with you; I believe most people only regret their choices and actions when the consequences deliver a crushing blow to their ego or personal lifestyle altogether. What if we lived in a world where we never had to answer for our actions? Let's be honest if we lived in a world where consequences didn't make us repent, how many people would be truly sorry for their actions? Acknowledging the hurt we caused others is very vital to our future growth process, and rebuilding our damaged relationships. Personally I struggled with acknowledging the hurt I caused others because I was selfish, and only cared about myself. I had what many might call massive pride issues which created a monster of doubt in my heart. Rory "Big 40" Atkins is famous for saying "a man's pride is the rope that hangs him in time." I like when he says this because it's a constant reminder to remember to keep my ego in personal check among other things. I remember the day Rory Atkins and I developed the idea of 7 Steps to Repair Unhealthy Relationships, which grew into a greater cause to many souls alike. Rory and I were brain storming during an early morning work out, in which we wanted to develop a program to help others rebuild and restore their unhealthy relationship. The results were without question D.R.D.C (Denver Reception Diagnostic Center) staff supported our vision and we made it come true.

Here is a poem I wrote a few years ago which paints a better picture on the subject at hand.

# Ego

They say
"Just say you're sorry"
I frown and look away
As if I would lay down my pride…
No one but my ego
Not today
*(Continued On Next Page)*

They want me to be humble
I mumble under my breath
"Just say you're sorry" they say
There's no one left
Broken by own discomforts
Telling myself something has to give
Dying is like a having a giant ego
And being scared to really live

"The corruption of the best is the worst of all"

# Refusing to Recognize the Truth

Recently, I spoke to this young man who found it in his best interest to make an excuse why his unhealthy relationship with his girlfriend didn't need any repairing. Clearly I could tell he was struggling with recognizing the truth in his own words, which is odd when you consider how many people refuse to acknowledge their faults. When we acknowledge our faults we grow to see the world from a realistic point of view instead of the candy coated perspective. I believe the hardest part about acknowledging the truth within ourselves is the fact we like to lie to ourselves. When we lie to ourselves it makes us feel better, pleasure freaks. It's almost like we are afraid to stare the truth in the mirror and see the monster we created. I can't tell you how many people I've met in prisons who were professional cone dodge ball champions at dancing around the truth. Every time I would speak with someone in prison I would say to myself here comes the bold face lie. The sad part about having to recognize the value in other people is sometimes you are disappointed by their actions or lack of effort. Do you remember when you were young and your mother or father explained to you how they were disappointed in your actions? The truth was your parents weren't only disappointed in your actions, but also disappointed in the fact you refuse to acknowledge your greatness at hand. Imagine a person with all the potential in the world, or an outstanding amount of talents. Now imagine this person refusing to acknowledge the greatness within them. Wouldn't that just drive you to know this person throws away opportunity the same way we throw away large quantities of food every year? The truth is we are sicken by anyone who refusing to acknowledge the truth when it blankly stares us in the face. When we really want to repair our unhealthy relationships we must first be willing to recognize the bold truth which never yields in life. The bold face truth is sometimes we are full of it, and refuse to recognize our daily nonsense from within. If you think I'm lying about the truth ask yourself if I'm talking about you in this passage? I was talking to a friend the other day about how to recognize when someone is telling you a lie. I told him "there's no way to notice when someone is telling you a lie." When it comes to recognizing the truth in others it's best to ask yourself why people lie in the first place. Once you discover why people lie, it will give you a better understanding on how to deal with those who choose to lie to you.

*"Those who lie for you will lie against you"*
**- -Unknown**

# Step Two: Accountability

The second step to repairing an unhealthy relationship is taking accountability for you role in the damage you've caused to the relationship. Taking account for your actions consist of never blaming others for your hurt/harm you personally caused them or the bond.

What stops you from taking accountability for the hurt and harm you caused to the bond?

_____
_____

Out of the following characteristics which one(s) caused the most damage to your relationship?

    Lying   Cheating   Manipulating   Domineering
    Abusive Behavior   Neglect   Lack of trust

Growing up I recall my house hold being loyal wresting fans. Just like many others in the south, wresting created a warm space in the hearts of many people. I even recall a teacher in my school stating to our entire class "in the south we have four things we love; God, family, football, and wresting. Anyway it wasn't long before my brothers and I became old enough to try certain wresting moves on one another. Imagine yourself being a genuine spectator of the greatest fake wresting match known to mankind. My brothers and I were so serious about the characters that we fought over who would be The Rock or Stone Cold Steve Austin, and trust me it got pretty ugly at times. It was as if we had our own little fight club (the first rule of fight club is you don't talk about fight club) see Fight Club starring Brad Pitt and Ed Norton. The reason why I mentioned this story is because I look at the state of my brothers and me today and say to myself where did we go wrong? It's like we aren't remotely as close as we use to be as young boys who simply enjoyed one another's company. If I had to acknowledge my role in the distance between my brothers and I, the word neglect would be the first one to speak upon. I neglect my bonds with my brothers for so many years, chasing success and feeling as if I didn't have time for them. Just like many others classified as workaholics, I put my family on the back burner in order to make myself successful. I don't deny it, and many of my relationships have suffered the same feat when it put up against the likes of my career. I acknowledge I have a tendency to put work before my family so I am always on the look out for when I am putting those close to me on the back burner. Would you say you put your family before your job or the other way around? Why? If you were to ask me why I put success before my family it's because I have certain of levels of fear when it comes to being labeled as mediocre and over looked in life. I'm not perfect but I try to be as honest as I can be to myself and others. It is very important to be honest with your loved ones even if telling the truth hurts their hearts or feelings. I personally hate letting people down or watching others grow a sense of disappointment in my actions. My dear friend Nicholas "Fingers" Pacheco and I were discussing our past one day, which presented a conversation about letting our loved ones down. While talking Nicholas said something very profound to me and I would like to share it with the world. He said "brother I let down a lifetime of people who loved me dearly, and didn't even know it because I couldn't see how I had developed a habit of suffering in life." By Nicholas sharing those words with me I felt truly privileged seeing how what he said summed up a lot of how I lived my life as well. I'm sure after reading this passage you'll probably have a point of relativity to express as well. I would say that is the beauty of expression, being able to relate to one another's pain and joy. (Selfishness) I met this young man while facilitating one of the 7 Steps to Repair Unhealthy Relationships classes the other day who made it a point to highlight his selfishness actions and how he deliberately his relationships out of the fear of losing his wife. I calmly sat there in my seat and listened as he explained how he cared for his wife, but did not trust her because he knew she had every reason to mistreat him the same way he mistreated her. So what he was actually saying to himself was his lack of trust stemmed from the likes of the hurt he caused his wife, generating an unhealthy level fear.

I believe selfishness is something everyone understands in their heart and mind, but the part that's difficult for our loved ones to understand is the reason why we are selfish at times. The truth is some people don't even recognize they are being selfish until someone brings it to their attention. Another truth is some people have been acting selfishly so long they've grown accustom to rolling over others with big tires. I recall a time when taking accountability presented a real challenge to my mindset. When it came to taking accountability I had major pride issues with saying I was wrong. Honestly saying I'm sorry felt like I was backing down, and I wasn't backing down from nothing at a very young dumb age. I learned that when I put my pride before my understanding, bad things happen. I can tell you it has been an entire journey battling my selfish pride, but I keep it in check the best I can.

The bold truth is most people don't expect much from themselves which becomes the underlining factors of their disappointment. You can usually find the masses believing in systems before they trust their own faith. I had several conversations with a dear friend of mine by the name of Selectman Bay on how people settle for less than what they are guaranteed in life. As I write these words I can hear his voice echoing in the back of my mind. "The moment we accept our true selves and not the image we created is the moment we'll see who we were destine to be." From his divine wisdom of growth I found what it means to reach another level of accountability within myself. I also found what it means to hold the ones closet to me to higher standards as well. I mean if you look at yourself in the mirror, would you expect your reflection to be doing something opposite of yourself? (I don't think you would.) When looking at your friends and family members, ask yourself if they reflect your actions and mind state? If they don't I wouldn't waste a lot of your time on them.

## Family...isn't just blood,
### but true love

The kind of love you don't have to second guess
With a warm heart
You just know they care
Afraid for you when times are grim
Brave for you when you are scared
Happy for you when you smile deep
Strong for you when you have to weep
Honest with you when you lie
Understanding when you seek why?
In your heart, they can never leave
Their souls talk to you
Make you believe
Walks with you
Saying "don't worry about who you should be, just be who you are."
 That's family
The ones who get on your last nerve
The ones who tell you what you truly deserve
The ones who laugh with you
The ones who laugh at you
The ones who challenge you
The ones who check your pride, and make you get back in line
The ones you can count on through thick and thin
The Chris Miller and Damon Davis kind
The ones who tell you to use your mind
The ones who you don't simply find anywhere
The ones I call my family no matter what

*"A human being is part of the whole, called by us the "universe," a part limited in time and space. He experiences himself, his thoughts and feelings, as something separated from the rest- a kind of optical delusion of his consciousness. This delusion is a kind of prison for us, restricting us to our personal desires and to affection for a few persons nearest to us. Our task must be to free ourselves from this prison by widening our circle of compassion to embrace all living creatures and the whole of nature in its beauty."*

-**Albert Einstein**

# Step Three: Honesty

The third step to repairing an unhealthy relationship is honesty. We must first be honest with ourselves and others in order to begin the healing process. Honesty is a vital step to understanding the people you hurt and yourself. For example, the person you may have hurt may not like being "lied" to. My best friend Patricia Riley has a pep pee about people lying to her, she truly hates lairs. I once asked her if she had to choose between a cheater and a liar as a mate which one would she choose. The answer I received from her made me laugh to my heart. She said she wouldn't choose either one, "throw them both away" she told me. The truth is no one likes to discover someone is being dishonest with them, especially someone you consider a loved one. To help you better understand notion, name something you would greatly dislike if someone were to do it to you?

_____

_____

Now picture, this someone is a person you care for dearly. Even though you care for about this person, how many times would you allow this incident to occur?

_____

_____

A funny story which highlights the point I'm trying to make is the time my cousin brought a bunch of candy from the store. I swear the moment we walked through the front of his mother's house she already knew to ask him if he had spent all his money on candy. I remember saying to myself how could she possibly know he brought candy at the store when she was at home. My cousin probably got nervous and froze up, telling her a lie before she could finish interrogating him. This lie infuriated her to the point of no return, and I could tell as I bolted out of the door like a bow legged impala. (I ran until my shoes came off). Sadly this was only one of many lessons I learned about lying that resulted in a close encounter. My dear friend Christopher Miller once told me "the best lie is one that doesn't get told." To better quote my beloved family member Patricia Riley, "you don't tell lies William, you just tell good stories!" I agree with her, as I fancy myself to be a walking motion picture. And the award for best lair of the year goes to… (Drum roll please). I believe a person has to grow out of lying, which means a person must get to the point where they don't have to lie about anything. If you were to ask yourself who in life has to lie? After you ask yourself who has to tell a lie, now put a face and a characteristic to the lie (who do you see?).

The moment you reach a comfortable point in your life where you don't feel you have to lie, steal, cheat, or dance around the truth; that's the moment you can say you're being honest with yourself. Think about it like this, if you heard Bill Gates got caught stealing from a local super market, I'm guessing it would be pretty hard to believe. The reason why it would be so hard to believe Bill Gates stole anything because everyone knows Bill Gates doesn't have to steal anything. Whenever we reach the same perspective Bill Gates or anyone who understands certain actions are beneath them, we'll act accordingly as well. I know that sounds pretty simple, but as humans we are the first to complicate a simple situation. Every situation we go through in life doesn't always have to have a complicated foil. I can honestly say I use to be the first person to strongly support doing things the hard way, but now I'm the first person to promote using one's mind and muscle to get things accomplished. If we take the time to realize how important honesty is to others and ourselves, we create a bond within ourselves and those who love us the most.

*"When you fancy yourself a better person, you are forced to act accordingly to your title"*
                              **-- William S. Graham**



*"We have to be utterly broken before we can realize that it is impossible to better the truth. It is the truth that we deny which so tenderly and forgivingly picks up the fragments and puts them together again".*
                              **-- Laurens Van der Post**

## Communicating Through Technology

Some people would agree technology is a form of communication, but others would challenge their ideologies by stating is technology the most affective way to communicate? I can't even lie to any of you when I say I'm torn between communicating through technology and traditional forms of expressing myself to others. Is it safe to say you are just like me, an emotional subject avoider? Are you the type of person who prefers to put off dealing with emotions and hard feelings that challenge the heart? Or maybe you were born during the digital era and were not shown how to communicate without technology. Would you rather send a sad face emoji to express how someone has made you feel bad then write out your true feelings? Here's a subject that has presented itself during my mentorship groups. As stated when choosing to break up with someone, should the news of the break up be face to face or through technology? If you were to ask me how I would conduct an important matter such as the heart, I would say it's particularly best to discuss them face to face.

## Lying to Yourself

This same time last year a very dear friend of mine by the name of Jeremiah Turner presented me with a challenging question. Jeremiah asked me how hurtful is lying to oneself compared to lying to others? I recall a lingering pause captivating the room before I responded to his question. I told him lying to oneself, from my perspective, is equivalent to being psychologically blind. I quickly added the ability to lie to your own self is far more detrimental to your well being than lying to others. When you lie to others, you are conscious of your ability to try and deceive them, but when you lie to your own self- your conscious level is tricking itself. (That's crazy but people do it everyday). You know as well as I do, when a person lies to themselves they are either full of crap or stuck in a state of denial. The truth is a lot of people destroy their relationships due to being stuck in a state of denial. Let's say you have a drug problem, and you refuse to acknowledge it but your significant other is begging for you to seek help. How long would you think it would take your significant other to get frustrated and leave you? As we know everyone has a breaking point they reach, and it's all over from there. I recommend you address your problems before your problems address you or something like that. Here is an exercise you should do when you have the proper time to yourself. First find a very clear mirror, and look directly into it. When you look into the mirror don't speak, just look at yourself. As you examine your eyes, your nose, your lips, and your face entirely —ask yourself what are some features about your face you admire and what are some features about your face you dislike? After you examine the features of your face, ask yourself if you are trust worthy? Do you have a trust worthy face? Remember its best to never lie to yourself, it only hurts you. A dear friend of mine by the name of Alex Manigo always says "people lie to their reflections all the time, and believe whatever people tell them to believe."

*"It's always best being straight forward when telling someone how you feel, how you think, and what you think about them."*

**Julie Rada- DU** PAI

## Step Four: Comprehension

The fourth step to repairing an unhealthy relationship is comprehension. By comprehending the effects of the bonds and how we damaged it, we truly understand we must take it upon ourselves to repair the bond. The power to mentally grasp what happens to us or during our altercations is the gift of truth given to ourselves. Ask yourself what caused the damage to the relationship(s) and what effects came there after?

Cause

_____
_____

Effect

_____
_____

If given the opportunity to repair the unhealthy relationship, how would you handle the situation differently?

_____

By the time I turned 13 years old I can honestly say I never thought I would have a normal kid's life. (As if to say a normal life makes you normal right). When you look at your life, you have to understand the humorous moments which are destine to occur no matter what. The moment I was able to laugh at how humorous life has the possibility to be, I grew like a wild flower on the side of the road.

When climbing a massive hill in your life don't forget to anticipate a slip or a fall down the way. How else are you suppose to test yourself or measure up to your greatest attributes if you're not forced to elevate beyond the level you know? Sometimes we see life as it is, raw and uncut, but the child in our hearts remembers a time when everything seemed to be at play. The power of comprehension is a gift bestowed upon us all to have, hold, and honor within our daily existence. The truth is if you don't know what something is capable of doing or being, you'll always fear it before you abuse it. When we consider the knowledge of mankind there are many examples of how we are infatuated with destroying things. The moment you are faced with two options –sink or swim (creation kicks in very fast.)

*"Everyday you have to be willing to work at the things you want and hold true. If you don't strive for the people and things you love, they definitely want strive for you"*
               **Ahmad Nelems**

## Humor

People don't accept me
They laugh at me
Say I should be like them
Not free
Running with the bulls
Sleeping among the flowers
Yelling from mountain tops
Laughing with cowards
Dancing with wolves
Throwing fire
Holding secrets
Chasing desires
Knowing truths
Balancing time
Learning to love
Staying behind
Searching to find
Lost diamonds in a mine
That's humorous

*"The unsatisfied soul is a thirsty grave yard of time"*

## Wear and Tear

As you may know it's no mystery to discover the wear and tear we place upon the things we own. Have you ever heard the old saying "sometimes the things you own eventually end up owning you?" That's definitely true when you take into consideration some of the things you own, and how you enjoy spending your time. The truth is as we enjoy the things we own, we're putting wear and tear on them as well. Let's take a brand new sweater from a high end department store for example. After you purchase this sweater, for some odd reason this same sweater becomes your favorite item of clothing to wear. You wear this favorite sweater of yours once a week, and you also wash this favorite sweater of yours once week. This form of wear and tear on your favorite sweater addresses the relationship and purpose you have with your favorite sweater on a daily basis. Boldly, we understand how different a sweater compares to a relationship but we also must acknowledge the wear and tear we put on our unhealthy relationships. If we were to examine the wear and tear we put on our relationships, is it safe to say we do it unconsciously? I believe we do. I know I can speak for myself when I say I loved things and used people, knowing it was wrong. The importance of remaining conscious when dealing with the emotions and feelings of others has to be something we must grow to appreciate. If we grow to appreciate the feelings of others, we elevate ourselves to another level of empathy. Having empathy for others, including our loved ones grants us the ability to understand how important our relationships truly are to us. The bold truth is most people feel family shouldn't have to earn our respect, which is a lie. No matter who you are or what you may feel for a person, just remember earning respect goes both ways. One of the most reoccurring events I've grown to discover when it comes to broken relationships is barrowing money from one another. What I mean by barrowing money from one another is people i.e. family members or friends lending money to one another, which never gets paid back. As you may know, whenever the money doesn't get paid back, it causes a tear in the bond. The lending party feels that the barrower doesn't respect the bond – causing a sense of separation. Have you ever felt as if you and your friends were in a different head space due to a disagreement? How did that make you feel? I'm guessing it made you feel a little upset or salty knowing something as small as a disagreement caused such a gash in your bond. I know many of my friends who don't barrow money of lend money to their friends or family members. I once asked them why they don't prefer to lend money to their family members or friends, and the answer I received was very profound. My friends calmly stated "if I never lend any money to my family members or friends/barrow, we'll never fall out over money.

When we take a close observation at the wear and tear placed upon our relationships we must never forget that no one has to endure our non-sense. At times we find that most people who tolerate non-sense are perceived to be weak or gullible, when that's not the case whole heartedly. The truth is people who tolerate the abuse of others, especially loved ones, just take a little longer to walk away. If I may quote a dear friend of mine, Danielle Hudson who always tells to cherish the things we call irreplaceable. It's a fact I've noticed how many people in relationships don't truly appraise love until they no longer have it.

*The test of a first-rate intelligence is the ability to hold two opposed ideas in the mind at the same time, and still retain the ability to function.*
**-F. Scott Fitzgerald**

# Step Five: Seeking Forgiveness

The fifth step to repairing an unhealthy relationship is seeking forgiveness. When we seek forgiveness, a sense of understanding calmly sweeps over us- just like peace. By seeking forgiveness we grow to understand the bonds that were broken and why the bond was so important to us in the first place. Not to add if you don't seek to forgive yourself and accept the results of thus findings you'll be stagnated in your own growth. There's many studies dedicated to the lack of forgiveness produces hatred in the heart, which develops into bitterness and possible terminal illness. Being remorseful about how you damaged the bond isn't always enough to repair the unhealthy relationship. You have to be willing to put forth the actions of change and efforts of truth. I remember being young with a heart full of unlawful actions to support my outlandish ideas. Anyway these same actions gave me a lot of lessons and blessings to draw from, and one of these lessons that comes to mind is understanding how powerful forgiveness is to every soul. Who have you hurt and would like them to forgive you?

_____
_____
_____
_____
_____

Who has hurt you and deserve your forgiveness?

## **Forgiveness Letter**

I come to you, asking for your forgiveness for




I understand that




My hopes are

*I thank you for giving me the time to express something weighing upon my heart and mind. Regardless of the results, I just want you to know I realized the amount of hurt I caused you, and I acknowledge the worth of our bond. Building up the courage to compose this passage wasn't an easy thing to do, but I felt compelled to do it because I realize how special you are to me. Thank you.*
*Oderint dum metuant [L]: let them hate, so long as they fear*
*-William S. Graham*

When it comes to forgiveness I'll be honest with you guys. I use to be the king of holding grudges and seeking revenge on people who hurt me or caused me harm. I recall a time when I use to take things so personal, I would make myself sick contemplating how to get them back. My beloved aunt once told me "you're so spiteful; you grind your teeth when you're sleeping!" I laughed at her comment at the time, but years later thought about the root of my problem and how to heal it. I know there are some individuals reading this who probably feel the same way I use to feel about seeking revenge on anyone who causes them hurt or harm. I understand you might feel as if you can't forgive them or pick up the phone and call them, just to talk. I wouldn't dare ask you to do such a thing if you're not ready to do that. The advice I would say to you is life is too short to be holding onto grudges that only hurt you in the end. At first you tell yourself by no means necessary will you ever forgive them for what they did to you? I can see you now sitting in your living room about to explode into a million pieces thinking about how they did you wrong. It's like they took a giant piece of your heart and put it in a blender to make smoothies out of your emotions. I get it! You're not anywhere close to being able to forgive them for what they did to you, depending on the level of the commitment, you may never forgive them. But understand its best not to seek vengeance upon someone who caused you ill will. Historically many cultures have retaliated against one another for actions deemed unforgivable. Clearly you will admit entire kingdom have been scorched to the ground behind retaliation. I remember as young boy I was addicted to gangster films, and I studied them religiously. I also recall taking visual notes as if I was due to be tested by some gangster academy who would give me a reward for my studies. Would you like to know something I learned from watching gangster films before I started living what I loved watching? I learned one of the main elements of a disagreement begins with an unlawful action taking place which promotes a swift retaliation. Then after both sides feel as if they've made their point, they have a sit down. The truth is a sit down is really just an open floor for all parties to air out their grievances and reach a compromise. (Sounds like something you need to do with someone over something that needs to get aired out right!) I'm not saying you should study gangster films like I did growing up, and by all means necessary don't ever live the lifestyle I choose in my earlier life, but you would agree a sit down must take place. A dear friend of mine once asked me is forgiving people who've harmed you or hurt you easier for some and difficult for others? Yes, forgiving people who harmed you or hurt you could be the most difficult thing you've ever had to do, but it doesn't mean it can't be done. It has been proven people forgive each other every day, and go off to live prominent lives. Then there's the cold hard truth which supports a large percentage of our daily arrest surround around ill will or some vendetta-like circumstances. How many times have you been watching a murder mystery show, only to say "the husband did it?" Or maybe it was the wife who tried to hire a hit man to murder her husband (I'm just saying). Remember the board game (Clue) where you didn't know who to trust because everyone seemed like a suspect? Indeed you see the point I'm trying to make when I say if I were you I wouldn't go around trying to get back at everyone who made you feel some type of way. I'll tell you right now, there aren't enough hours in a day for the likes of wrong doers and enemies. How does the old saying go, I might forgive but I'll never forget. I know that's quite contradictive of me seeing how I haven't lived a perfect life myself. I'll be honest with you guys, I have to ask my kids for forgiveness as you read this because I has been absence from their lives. But before you stone me to death please know I have been in prison since they were born. Also you should know I truly dislike people who make excuses for their mistakes in life. With all that said I will say my prison sentence didn't excuse for why I wasn't there for my kids during hard times. I use to tell myself I would write letters explaining the situation once they got older, but I put it off until later. As many people would expect later turned into thereafter, and thereafter turned into I don't know if I should write the letters at all.

William Graham

# I'm Sorry

I recall as a child doing very devious things throughout my days. I would plot and scheme on my teachers and care givers with a grand sense of mental warfare. I'm sure if army generals could have seen my tactics, they would agree my strategy was far from juvenile. But like most wet behind the ears schemers I would make tiny mistakes that eventually resulted in me getting caught. After being caught for whatever spoiled plot I could fathom up I would then start my I'm sorry speeches which were very heart felt (wink, wink). Here's the thing about saying you're sorry to the one's you offend or cause harm too. Do you really mean it when you say (I'm sorry) to the ones you offend or cause harm too? The reason why I ask this question is because honestly whenever I would do devious things as a child, and then get in trouble for the things I had done, I was never sorry for my actions. I was sorry I got caught, but never was I sorry for my actions. This childish like behavior became my calling card throughout my young adult hood as well. I would feel shame and guilt just like many others who apologize with a fist full of tears, but I was not truly sorry in my heart. I would cheat on my girlfriends throughout my young relationships, playing mind games like a war game of chess. Then like you expected I would be the first one saying I'm sorry and giving out gifts like Santa Claus. Are you someone who uses the words (I'm sorry) as a weapon instead of a state of repentance? I know I use to be a master at using the words I'm sorry to get others to forgive me, only to hurt them later.

# Step Six: Listen to Understand

The sixth step to repairing an unhealthy relationship is active listening to the person(s) you've harmed or hurt to understand their point of view in the whole matter. By allowing the wounded party to express themselves about the hurt that occur you empower the relationship, and one other to see different perspectives (feel as well). I read in this one book, the power to be heard and understood is what the human soul truly seeks in life. So you can understand how important it is for their voice to have power in your life, and in your heart. This same power has the ability to prevent the chances of the hurt occurring again. Failing to listen or allow the damaged party to be understood is detrimental to the relationship causing vital pieces of communication to be lost. When we use proper listening skills, called active listening skills, we can significantly reduce misunderstandings, create a safe space for vocalizing feelings and truly help you and your loved ones understand each other better.

Do me a beautiful favor in your thoughts in you may. Picture a room full of people talking at once, and no one listening to one another. Can you picture this room in your mind? What if this room was a company you work for, or maybe you already work for a company of people who only talk and never listen? How would or how does that feel? I'm guessing it sucks huh! Many people would agree on how important active listening is to all, especially those who have bad blood with one another.

## I'm Dying

Looking out this window
In a place called home
Floating through the room (silence)
Time ha! Ha! Ha!
Reflection in the mirror, a ghost
Where is purpose?
I loss it
Pain matches cardboard feelings
Air stiff and pale
I wish I could breathe…exhale and inhale
Looking inward and outward
Chalky food gets chewed slowly
Pills lines designed to make us dance
Please remind me again
Why I'm dying with this glance
Of nothing but a window

This poem was written to highlight a heart felt story a guy told me a few years back. The guy's story begins with his abusive father beating his mother on Christmas Eve, and breaking her leg. Throughout his life, he went off to war, got married, and had children himself. The guy admitted to me he wasn't always the most pleasant to be around. Many later years he found himself in a prison infirmary dying of lung cancer. I was the only one there as he passed away, with my pen in hand. The lesson I learned from the older gentleman was no matter what happens to us in life, good or bad, we have to be willing to grow pass the hurt in order to heal those around us. As I spoke with the dying old man, I realized how at times we tend to over look the things that truly matter in life. Love really matters in life. Family really matters in life. Growth really matters in life. Understanding really matters in life. Loyalty really matters in life. Learning to trust others really matters in life. Time really matters in life. The moment you ask yourself what really matters to you, is the moment your heart inherits its true desires. Have you ever heard the old saying "if you think small-you get small results?" This works the same way when we take a close look at our relationships, which sometimes are unhealthy and in need of repairing. Note to self: don't be so eager pity the uncommitted people of the world.

# Hesitation

Without hesitation I say sometimes you have to put a healthy amount of space between you and the people you love in order to truly grow. I know that bit of advice sounds quite opposite when you consider a guide book about repairing unhealthy relationships. But one of the key components of repairing unhealthy relationships is the ability to be able to recognize you are in an unhealthy relationship. Have you ever heard the phase "you can't see the forest despite the trees?" What this quote means is sometimes we overlook or simply fail to see the bigger picture due to our limited views. The reason why they call it a bird's eye view is because you get a full view of what is perceived to be true. I'm not ashamed to admit I spent a large majority of my life struggling with many toxic relationships. Every time I would get out of a toxic relationship, I would look up to discover myself in another one. The part that makes no sense is I knew my relationships were toxic to me, but I continued to swim in them out of fear of losing the ones closet to my heart. If I were to tell you I repeated this process over and over again until it became first nature to me, I'm sure it wouldn't shock you. The same way, we as humans, smoke cigarettes, drink hard liquor, and take drugs- toxic relationships are just as harmful as other high risk activities. I can honesty speak from experience when I say you should never hesitate to distant yourself from any toxic relationship you may encounter. Just remember when it comes to any toxic relationship its always best to acknowledge the problem, address the problem face to face, understand the problem, and don't hesitate to get away from the problem once it becomes too toxic to bare.

**Aegri somnia- a sick man's dreams (Latin)**

*"That's Latin daring; it seems Johnny Ringo here is an educated man…now I really hate him!"*
- Doc Holiday quote from the movie Tombstone.

# Step Seven: Patience

The seventh step to repairing an unhealthy relationship is patience. By giving the bond the proper time it needs to develop back into a healthy relationship they're able to see growth in you and the bond grants them comfort. This same comfort allows them the proper time to heal and possibly forgive you for whatever occurred. This is not to say that they weren't wrong as well, but this is you making taking the first steps toward repairing the relationship(s). Also a personal note to self is sometimes people do not instantly forgive us for what occurred, which is fine. Keep in mind this occurs in broken bonds and you will grow from their rejection as well. Do not let this discourage you from trying to repair the unhealthy relationship or being conscious of future mistakes and habits having the power to repeat the same damage over and over again.

I remember when I use to cause hurt/harm to my loved ones in the past, I would be the first one trying to heal the wound like I didn't cause it. That's like someone stabbing you in the chest, and driving you to the hospital, asking "who did this to you?" I'm sure I can see the faces of many saying now "you did this to me!" I'm sure you would agree if a person easily forgives you for a treacherous action, it makes you wonder about their level of commitment to the bond or if they're planning their vengeance already. I would say people who are slow to forgive you are probably struggling with the fact they never thought you, of all people would cause them hurt or harm. You have to accept you may have hurt them deeply to their core, and now they are still in a state of shock. I would say give them some time to heal, and understand you created your situation and they are simply reacting to the hurt you caused them. Like we stated in the honesty chapter, you have to be willing to be honest with yourself even while they are healing. If you find yourself getting upset with the person you hurt or caused harm to, just remember who you should be actually mad at for damaging the bond in the first place. Here is a bit of knowledge I learned a few years ago. Despite what anyone has ever told you, life is a bully. If you allow it to beat you down every chance you get, never standing up to it, you'll just be a human punching bag. But if you stand up to life a few times, you'll discover "life" will think twice before throwing a punch your way. Or you can keep crying and complaining how you were dealt a bad hand in life. (Tiny violins in the background) I once knew this guy who wanted everything instantly. No matter what it was, he hated waited for it. One day he was walking through a garden and seen a piece of fruit not quite ripe, but he couldn't wait so he plucked it from its branches anyway. As a result of eating early fruit, he became terribly sick for several days thereafter. Is it safe to say you have a difficult time practicing patience in your daily life? How would you say you developed this lack of patience? Does your lack of patience stem from being spoiled as a child who never waited for anything in your house hold? Or is it something more in depth going on in that complex mind of yours? Ask yourself: Do I practice good patience? It's always best to be honest with yourself, lying to yourself is like pouring yourself a glass of poison and calling it champagne. Here is a perspective I adopted many years ago which gave me develop a greater sense of patience. During my years of discovering truth I learned that everything has a proper time and place in my life. In this day and age a lot of people worry themselves to death trying to manage time or be somewhere important. As I look at life from a different perspective, my mind explores what it means to accept the things that happen in life, and deny the things that aren't meant for me.

*"If you rush throughout your entire life, you'll grow to accept things they leave instantly"*
                                                    **-Susan Gomez**

# Now What!

As you examine your new tools of growth and understanding, there's a question formulating in your mind (what now?) I must say that is a very good question if you want to do something about it. You see it's clear to see most people understand things as well as anyone, but only a few people apply things. The truth is most people after reading this guide will revert back to not taking actions or responsibility for their part in damaging their bonds. If you are this type of person, understand you can't be a coward all your life. Yeah, you read that correctly, I called you a coward at heart. If the shoes fit your feet, walk a mile in them my friend. But if you are different and bold hearted than you know what you have to do right? When I say now what? Please believe that is an open challenge to all those who long to repair an unhealthy relationship or change their perspectives. I'm pretty sure you've heard the day old saying "team work makes the dream work." And without a shadow of doubt we all discover how true this quote actually equates in our personal and business lives. But I also prompt the question of what does it mean to be a team mate? How do you view your significant other and your children? The reason why I asked how you see your significant other and children governs how you view yourself as a team mate. What role would you say you play in your immediate family? Are you the team captain? Are you the first person in your family to show up and the last to leave? Or are you the back up quarter back? Maybe you're the person on the team who passes out water to everyone on the team. Now understand all of these roles are important to the team, but why does one feel more important than the other? Do you feel important in your role as a father, husband, son, daughter, mother, wife, friend, etc. etc.? How important would you say you feel at your job? I know a lot of people who say "I hate my job and all the people I work with as well." (Aren't you a social butterfly in the cubical)? The hard core truth is everyone will not like you, this we know to be true. It's not about getting everyone to like you, but we must always desire to understand is our own faults and flaws. What I mean by this is, your boss may be a grade "A" flap jack, but do what you have to do to make the situation favorable for you. (And trust and believe the word favorable doesn't mean what some of you dirty minded people are thinking about.) What I'm trying to say is if you put your best foot forward and make it happen for yourself you'll grow into the person you desire to be.

"When choosing a position in life, make sure you're not just doing it because you need a title"
-Terry Mosley Jr.

# The 6 R's of Repair

If you were to ask anyone who has ever made a mistake in their lifetime, surely they would agree making a mends is one the hardest things to do. But I question, why is it so hard to make a mends for some people? I can't speak for anyone else, but I can speak for myself when I say mending broken bonds were hard for me because I had major pride issues. I recall many times when my pride would stand in my way, separating me from grand opportunities in my life. I use to tell myself I wouldn't allow my pride to destroy my chances and opportunities in life, but every time something challenging would come up I would shoot myself in the foot. I learned very fast I couldn't allow my pride to hinder my growth if I wanted to get ahead in life, and build healthy relationships. I also pay homage to my older brother Ronald Frye, who is a very humble man with true vision. When it comes to putting my pride to the side, I can't tell you how many times Ronald has given me a grand perspective on life. He once told me "people aren't stupid as you think they are little brother, they know the difference between good material and bad material." What my brother was telling me was if you see yourself as good material then others will see you as good material as well, and if you are able to recognize bad material – you'll save yourself a lot of time in headaches and heartaches. The advice my older brother, Ronald Frye gives me is what I like to call divine wisdom from a modern day scholar. The 6 R's of repair act as a guide to highlight our paths of restoring our unhealthy relationships. The 6 R's of repair are respect, reliability, reasoning, reparation, responsibility, and rebuilding. Each one of the 6 R's of repair plays a very vital role in our lives, especially when it comes to our unhealthy relationships. The truth is when we examine the 6 R's of repairing an unhealthy relationship we must be willing to see the process through, and not give up. If we take a hard look at how important each ® is in our lives, we'll develop growth within ourselves as well. It can't be that simple you say to yourself! Yes, it is my friends. The truth is when you heal others, you heal yourself as well. Let's take a look at the 6 R's and compare how vital they are in our lives, this will tell us how vital they are to others. Have you ever heard the term "do unto others what you want done unto you?" I didn't make that up, it's in the bible. But to those who need a simple break down read this part very slowly. If you don't like getting shot, don't go around shooting other people. If you don't like for people to steal things from you, don't go around town like I use to do robbing people. Here's one for you to chew on. If you don't like for your significant other to sleep around town with every hot rod with a pretty smile then you shouldn't be doing it either. Some would say respect in your relationships is everything, and I would agree whole heartedly. No matter how much money you may have or how pretty you are, you have to establish respect in your daily relationships if you want them last. Learning to respect others is a lesson I had to grow into over time. I can recall many of my relationships ending over the lack of respect I displayed to them. If you don't have respect in your relationship, it's like planting flowers and stepping on them the next day.

One of the 6 R's of repair essentially involves showing respect for your loved ones and yourself. During my years of speaking with individuals who informed me of the lack respect between their loved ones and themselves, I discovered something profound. I discovered how most people don't feel they have to respect their loved ones the same they would have to respect their friends or boss at work. Upon this discovery I was forced to ask myself have I ever exploited the respect of anyone deemed a family member or close acquaintance? The answer I discovered was yes I have exploited the respect of the ones closet to me. I actually had to learn to respect the ones closet to me in order for us to have fruitful encounters with one another. I also learned having respect for others, especially those closet to us, creates an esteem sense of honor between us and our loved ones. I know you probably are reading this passage saying to yourself "I've never exploited the respect of my loved ones." Are you sure you want to go there before I explain to you how most people don't even know they are being disrespectful to the ones closet to them. It's not your fault totally. This doesn't make you a scum bag by exploiting your family members or using them to be honest. Sadly to say everyone uses everyone in some way or another, which is the truth. Like for example you remember when your mother and father would make you baby-sit your little brothers or sisters so they could have old people date night? Did you get paid to watch your little brothers and sisters? No you did not #you got used. Most people say no harm-no foul when it comes to little things like not paying back small pieces of money or forgetting to return your best friend's favorite red sweater. When we consider the levels of respect which should be shown to our loved ones we must always remember to communicate with them and not take the love their for granted. Like for instance if your mother puts her foot down on you doing drugs and wants you to get clean, don't play around with her feelings. The reason why your mother is so passionate about you being clean is because she doesn't want you to make the same mistakes she made or allow drugs to destroy your life. You have to respect her wishes and try to get your life together as best as you can. The ability to have and share respect with the ones closet to you will grant you a gift of understanding and truth. At the moment you may feel that you have respect for your loved ones, which could be true, or you could be like most people (using and abusing) the ones you love. Another (R) of repairing an unhealthy relationship is realization. The moment we realize how important relationships are to us is the moment we'll cherish them accordingly. If you were to ask the average person what does the word relationship mean to them I bet a lot of people would be stuck trying to figure it out. It's no mystery to discover many people have no idea what a relationship actually entails. I always like to say the moment we realize how important our relationships are to us is like the moment we discover puberty. Our relationships help us grow up and challenge us to be better in our everyday lives. The other four R's of repairing an unhealthy relationship are reliability, reconciliation, responsibility, and rebuilding. If you had to put these in order to repair your unhealthy relationship, which one would you start with first?

*"Every wise person should seek out another wise person to balance their growth"*

                    -Sean J. Marshall formally known as "SD"
                    Author of "The Get-down and Count Bandit"

# 7 Steps to Repair Unhealthy Relationship
## (Interface)

At this point we've reached a marvelous exit with high hopes toward the future of healthy relationships. In all decency I figured it would be good in order to leave you with a piece of my soul to take with you on your journey. As you may have discovered by now, maintaining relationships isn't for the faint of hearts. The bold truth is sometimes we take our relationships for granted, very unaware of their true value. The beloved Latoya Andrews describes relationships as gardens which forever need attendance. The underlining factor in her description connects the responsibilities of having a relationship to the desire to maintain one. Do you remember the first time you begged your parents for a puppy? You were so excited to get the puppy you never even considered the responsibilities which came with having your own puppy. The moment you grew to accept all the responsibilities that accompanied having your own puppy you were more than happy to negate these same responsibilities to someone else. When we look at the practice of our own cars, the same negligence takes place daily. Do you remember when your car had that new car smell? I imagine you flying down the highway with a giant smile own your face singing Brittany Spears or Backstreet Boys in your new car. 7 years later, how did you feel about that same car? If I had to guess I would say you're probably thankful to have daily transportation in your life, but you don't admire your care the same way you use to value it. I believe we tend to treat our relationships the same way eventually. When we first get involved in certain relationships we treat them with a higher level of value that diminishes over time. I wonder why we lose interest in the things we attain and get upset when someone threatens to take the thing we're suppose to cherish away from us. Christopher Miller said "it is in our nature as humans to take things for granted, even the things we love dearly." The question fulminating in everyone's mind is how do we cure ourselves of such a spoiled point of view? I would say losing the things we're suppose to be cherishing is enough punishment, but the critics would say I'm being too soft on the masses. They want to see you burn! Now me personally I wouldn't go that far, but I would recommend you explore the value of every relationship you encounter. The great motivational speaker Travis Barnes is notorious for asking people to evaluate their self worth through the eyes of a higher power. I second that notion by adding I believe once we grow to understand the value of our relationships; we'll treat them like they're supposed to be treated. How do you know if you're in an unhealthy relationship or not? It's evident but not always clear to see if you're an unhealthy relationship or not. Most people consider themselves blessed to have others to call family and friends, and this blessing sometimes acts as curse against them. Like for example let's say you have a brother who refuses to move out of your apartment. You want to charge him rent, but he doesn't have a job. You say to yourself "he's my brother and I love him so I'm not going to be that hard on him." Let's say two years later your degenerate brother fails to show any sign of being normal again. One day you get tried of his nonsense and kick him out of your apartment. As you would guess this pisses him off and now he will not speak to you. At first you might feel pretty guilty about treating your brother the way you had to treat him, but those feelings will go away when you grow to understand you were helping him grow up as well. The power of having healthy relationships is just like eating healthy on a daily basis. If you were to look at your unhealthy relationships like bad eating habits, would it be safe to say you aren't surprised when the doctor gives you bad news every check up? I believe relationships are the same way, people having to make healthy choices over bad choices. As I leave you in thought I state "high hopes are granted to the ones who long to discover hidden truths." Thank you for traveling this beautiful journey with me, I salute you and I honor your growth. Take care of yourselves and each other.

## About the Book

7 Steps to Repair Unhealthy Relationships presents a gripping approach toward bond building, and overcoming damaging relationships. The truth about relationships is we all long to be more fruitful in our everyday relationships, and live a perfect harmonic life. Sometimes we find it difficult to maintain our daily relationships with balance and truth. Is there a relationship you long to repair, but find it hard to make a mends with the hurt you've caused or felt? 7 Steps to Repair Unhealthy Relationships challenges you to overcome your fears with the courage to do exactly what desire to do (produce healthy relationships.) Graham reluctantly shares thoughts with the reader as you gather a feel good approach toward truth and enlightenment.

## About the Author

Mr. William S. Graham wears many hats, and prides himself on growing beyond the flower pots of the world. Graham is a 7 times published author with books like Hurt People…Hurt People, The Locksmith of Love, A Guide to Understanding Your Mate and Yourself A Little Bit Better, Get Off The Tricycle, and many more to acknowledge. Graham is also the resident poet of Colorado's first and only prison podcast lead by the undeniable Dr. Ashley L. Hamilton entitled (thisiswithin.com). During his off days Mr. Graham donates his time mentoring and sharing thoughts with younger and divine individuals like himself. Mr. Graham quotes "relationships are the cornerstone of our hearts and the feeding source of our souls."

7 Steps to Repair Unhealthy Relationships

William Graham

# 7 Steps to Repair Unhealthy Relationships

William Graham

7 Steps to Repair Unhealthy Relationships

William Graham

# 7 Steps to Repair Unhealthy Relationships

William Graham

7 Steps to Repair Unhealthy Relationships

William Graham

7 Steps to Repair Unhealthy Relationships

William Graham

7 Steps to Repair Unhealthy Relationships

William Graham

7 Steps to Repair Unhealthy Relationships

William Graham

www.ingramcontent.com/pod-product-compliance
Lightning Source LLC
Chambersburg PA
CBHW071510070526
44578CB00001B/494